Pet Shop

So you want to get yourself a pet?
Well, you've come to the right place,
I've got just the group of animals
To put a broad smile on your face.

Here's a green anaconda
Straight from the Amazon.
She'll be happy if you feed her
With a deer or a caiman.

I've got alligators from the Everglades,
A crocodile from the Nile,
You surely can't resist those tears,
Or that inviting smile?

4

I have two poison dart frogs
From the jungles of Peru.
I bet this blue-ringed octopus
Is just the thing for you.

How about a box jellyfish?
A coyote? A brown bear?
A male komodo dragon?
Here's the female, take the pair.

I know you'd like this red-backed spider
Or this vampire bat.
What did you say? You'd rather have
A little dog or cat?

Sorry, we don't have that.

SOLD

Cat

Tail swisher
Bowl fisher
Night howler
Garden prowler
Milk lapper
Bird trapper
Tray filler
Rat killer
Tree hopper
Fur dropper
Fish eater
Mouse beater
Wool tangler
Kitten dangler
Collar wearer
Rabbit scarer
Roof walker
Moon talker
What's that?
The cat.

The Mouse's Song

If there is a mouse you are longing to please,

Give him cheese,

Give him cheese.

If you want to put a small mouse at his ease,

Give him cheese,

Give him cheese.

Don't hug him, don't kiss him, don't give him a squeeze,

Don't tickle his nose, it will just make him sneeze,

Don't feed him on parsnips, or porridge, or peas,

Give him cheese,

Give him cheese,

Give him cheese.

Confused Earthworm

It's not a he or a she,
Yet it's both him and her.
Should we call it "miss" or "mister"?
Which would it prefer?
It feeds on rotting leaves and soil,
But what is rather odd
Is that you'll often find it hanging
From the end of a fishing rod.

Slug

Trail blazer
Garden grazer
Slime slider
Leaf rider
Horn waver
Cabbage craver
Frog hater
Bird baiter
Night sneaker
Path streaker
Wall crawler
Seedling mauler
Night walker
Lettuce stalker
Hole plug
Slimy slug.

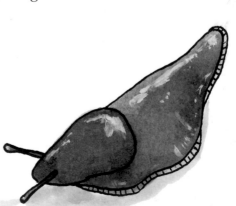

Snail

I'm in no hurry,
I'll take my time,
You go on ahead,
For this is quite a climb.
I'll take it slow
Along this track,
It's hard to go fast
With your house on your back.

Army Ants

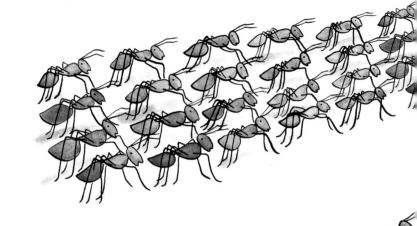

Here comes the army,
Tramp! Tramp! Tramp!
Guess where this army
Is setting up camp?

Charging through the windows,
Climbing through the doors,
Here comes the army
By twos and fours.

Here comes the army,
Tramp! Tramp! Tramp!
Guess where this army
Is setting up camp?

This army is hungry,
This army is mean,
This army is one big
Eating machine.

Here comes the army,
Tramp! Tramp! Tramp!
Guess where this army
Is setting up camp?

It's feeding on cockroaches,
Mice and rats.
You'd better leave your homes,
Take your dogs and cats.

Here comes the army,
Tramp! Tramp! Tramp!
Guess where this army
Is setting up camp?

Take your cows and goats,
Take your chickens too.
Run! For this army
Will even eat you!

Here comes the army,
Tramp! Tramp! Tramp!
Guess where this army
Is setting up camp?

Here comes the army,
Tramp! Tramp! Tramp!
Here's where this army
Is setting up camp!

13

Last Night I Saw a Hedgehog

Last night I saw a hedgehog
Hiding near the shed,
I caught him, put him in a box,
And fed him cheese and bread.

He curled up in the corner,
Gave a little squeak,
And I thought I saw a tiny tear
Rolling down his cheek.

So I put him back down by the shed,
And watched him scamper off to bed.

Squirrel in Winter

I know it's buried here somewhere,
It was underneath a tree,
But now the trees have lost their leaves,
They look the same to me.

I know it's buried here somewhere,
But it's nowhere to be found,
I can't tell where I made the hole
With this white stuff on the ground.

I know it's buried here somewhere,
And I'm looking high and low,
For I need to find my treasure
Before it starts to grow.

I know it's buried here somewhere,
On this side of the hut,
Why is it every cold time,
I always lose my nut?

15

I Don't Think Sheep Like Me

I don't think sheep like me,
I know they don't care
To have me around them,
Or anywhere near.

Whenever they see me,
Whether close by or far,
They turn their backs to me
And all shout out, "Bah!"

I went to the farm gate
And leant on the bar,
Quite polite, said, "Good morning,"
They turned and cried, "Bah!"

"Bah!"
Why do they hate me?
"Bah!"
What did I do?
"Bah!"
Why don't they like me?
I just wish I knew.

I don't know who those sheep
Think that they are,
To look so angrily
At me and cry, "Bah!"

The next time I see them,
Those four-legged blankets,
I'll say, "Bah! To you too,"
And see how they like it.

Loner

The tortoise won't have house parties,
Or invite friends round for fun,
For he likes to keep his own company,
And lives in a house for one.

He doesn't keep a helper,
A pet or a garden gnome,
And it hurts him that he cannot say,
"Tell them I'm not at home."

Sometimes he'd like to stay in bed,
Or laze around all day,
And leave a sign for visitors,
"Sorry, I've gone away."

But he knows he cannot be like folks,
Who like to potter about,
And leave a note pinned to their door
Saying, "I have just popped out."

So he'll pull his head into his home,
And he won't answer if you come callin',
Though everyone knows for certain
That he's permanently "in".

Greedy Goat

My goat eats anything,
Paper, cardboard, bits of string,
Apple pips or orange peel,
To goat it's just another meal.

Goat eats baskets, nibbles clothes,
Dolls and teddies, she'll eat those.
She took my pyjamas the other day,
I yelled, but she ate them anyway.

Aunt Rebecca's brand new hat,
Greedy goat said, "I'll have that!"
But even goat won't eat broccoli,
So why are you feeding it to me?

20

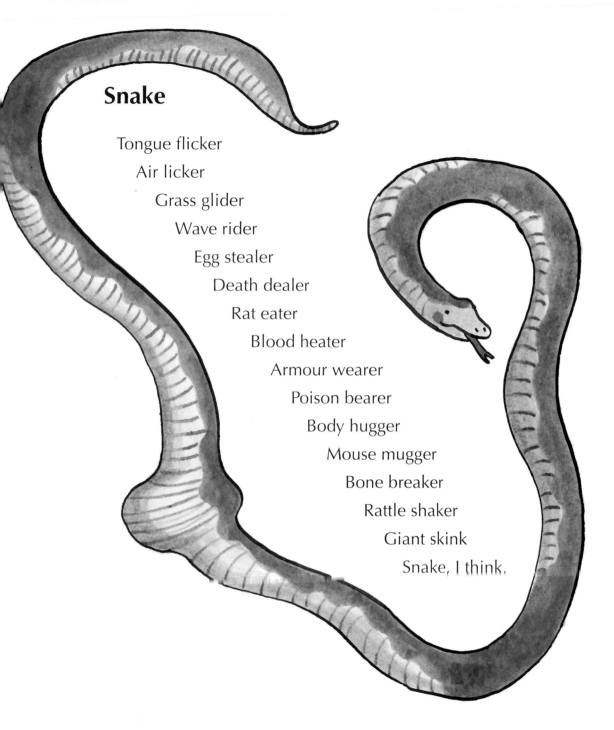

Snake

Tongue flicker

Air licker

Grass glider

Wave rider

Egg stealer

Death dealer

Rat eater

Blood heater

Armour wearer

Poison bearer

Body hugger

Mouse mugger

Bone breaker

Rattle shaker

Giant skink

Snake, I think.

Snake in the Grass

The snake cannot be trusted,
Sliding through sand and sea,
Sneaking through the bushes,
Or slithering round a tree.

For when you least expect it,
He'll raise his head and strike,
His fangs dripping with venom,
Pierces like a spike.

He'll often kill at random,
Not just the things he'll eat,
Like fish and snails and worms
And mostly anything with feet.

Some snakes will hug you, not in love,
But to squeeze you free of life,
Some will even eat their family,
Mother, sister, wife.

You'll often find this serpent,
Curled up beneath a stone,
Wondering why he has no friends,
And is always on his own.

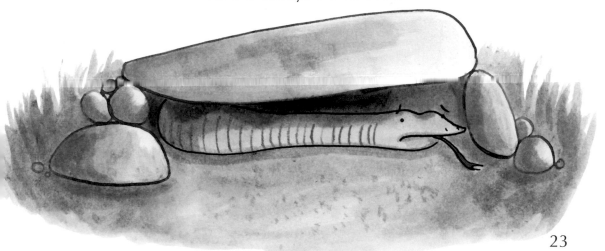

School Visitor

There's a monitor lizard in the cupboard,
Behind the teacher's chair,
And no one in the class knows
How that lizard got in there.

Perhaps she's planning to send her kids
To learn to read and write,
To learn their sums and ABC
And when and what to bite.

She may have come to see the teachers
To check which is best or worst,
She won't be impressed with ours,
For she's screaming fit to burst.

Perhaps she's here to join our class,
Perhaps the headmaster's sent her,
Maybe she'll sit in the front desk
And be our class monitor.

She's sent our teacher into a fit,
Given the caretaker a headache,
But I hope she stays around a while,
I love this longer break.

Hippo Speak

If you should meet a hippo
As he comes out to feed at dusk,
And he opens up his massive mouth,
And shows to you his tusks,

Before you nod and smile at him,
And say a warm "hello",
Before you reach to shake his hoof,
There's something you should know.

He's not about to sing or smile,
This hippo is not yawning,
He's not telling you he's tired,
He is giving you a warning.

He's got a nasty temper
And weighs well over a ton,
So when he opens wide his mouth,
It's time for you to RUN!

African Elephant

He's the largest living animal
And the heaviest on the land,
He rips up huge trees by the root
And snaps them like a wand.

The ground shakes where he travels,
Like a mountain rumbling by,
The forest bows before him,
Nothing's above him, except the sky.

Even the king of the jungle
Stands back to let him pass,
And people gaze in wonder,
At his power, might and mass.

This animal is an awesome sight,
He's built like a small house,
And yet this mighty elephant
Is frightened of a mouse.

The Lion Lay Still in the Zoo

The lion lay still in the zoo,
And dreamt of forests and streams.
The cage was sparkling and new,
The lion lay still in the zoo.
The people who crowded his view,
Tried to rouse him with shouts and with screams,
But the lion lay still in the zoo,
And dreamt of forests and streams.

Hyena

The hyena has a fearsome laugh,
And a most disgusting diet,
If you should see one in a shop
I'd advise you not to buy it.

The Wild Geese

The wild geese are flying south,
Where do they go?
Circling then turning about,
Row upon row.
The sun is warm, the sky is clear,
No sign of storm clouds anywhere,
But they are flying as if they fear
There will be snow.

The wild geese are flying straight,
Wings wide, and fleet,
Over meadow and farmyard gate,
Over city street.
They do not stop to build a nest,
They hardly stop to eat or rest,
As if they hear from out the west
The footsteps of sleet.

The wild geese are flying high,
Orange beak to tail,
A feathered V in the autumn sky,
Following an unseen trail.
Not in huddle or untidy sprawl,
But in tight formation, big and small,
And in each urgent wild goose call,
Is a warning of hail.

The wild geese are flying fast,
Like bullets through the air.
They tell the hedgehogs as they go past,
"Time to prepare!
Time to make a home that's warm,
Where you can sleep through each snowstorm."
They tell the swallows, "Time to swarm,
Winter is near."

The Owl

Who will feed my chicks tonight?
Who? Who? Who?
Who walks about in the pale moonlight?
Who? Who? Who?

Perhaps a mouse, perhaps a vole,
Perhaps a juicy bat,
Perhaps a mole has left his hole,
My children would like that.

Who'll run too slow from my sharp claws?
Who? Who? Who?
Who'll find their way into our jaws?
Whoo? Whoo? You!

Swift

A swift sleeps on the wing,
Now that's a peculiar thing.
Wouldn't he sleep sounder with his head
On a bed?

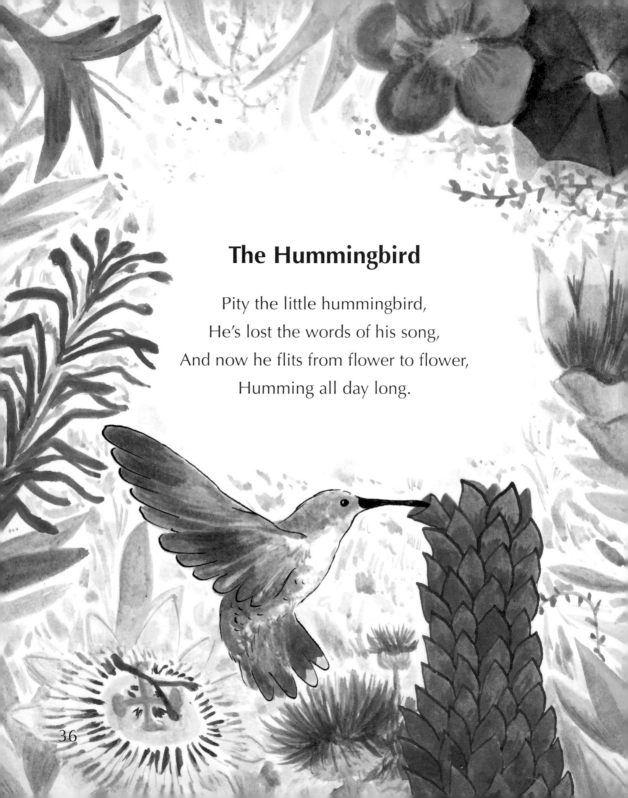

The Hummingbird

Pity the little hummingbird,
He's lost the words of his song,
And now he flits from flower to flower,
Humming all day long.

Seaside Bandit

Seagulls are supposed to fish,
Diving in the sea,
So why does this one sit and wait
To steal my chips from me?

The Dogfish

The first thing you should know about the dogfish,
Is it's not a fish, it's a shark.
The next thing you should know about the dogfish,
Is its bite is worse than its bark.

Octopus

The octopus has eight legs,
That's more than I would choose,
She must have such a hard time
Shopping for new shoes.

The octopus has eight hands,
It's so that she can bounce
Balls, skip and hug her mum,
And play catch all at once.

Does anyone know for certain
If the octopus's eight things
Are legs or hands or tentacles,
Or maybe tails or wings?

39

Whale Alert

Teacher said, "Research an animal, in the sea, the air, the ground,"
I chose to find out about the whale and this is what I found.

The whale is peaceful, the whale is smart,
The whale's got a song that could melt your heart.

Whales can't taste, and whales can't smell,
But whales can hear extremely well.

A whale that's singing – folk who know whales say –
Can be heard by others a hundred miles away.

A whale talks with a whistle, a squeak or a click,
Though he's big as a mountain, a whale's very quick.

They have no teeth, so they cannot chew,
And live on fishy things smaller'n me and you.

They never hurt people, so I'm sad to know
That people could treat the poor whale so.

They hunt him for his meat, for his oil and bone,
They will not leave the whale alone.

In just 50 years, two million have died,
Each with a harpoon growing from its side.

One day, there may be no more whales,
Except those living in fairy tales.

Fairy tales are good places for fairy folk to be,
But whales would be happier living in the sea.

41

You Can't Give Measles to a Shark

You can't give measles to a shark,
He will not catch your cold,
And he will not get tummy ache
If you feed him fish with mould.

You cannot make him catch the flu,
Or mumps or chickenpox,
He will not ask for herbs or pills,
From out your medicine box.

He'll not be struck by polio,
Or sickness of the liver,
No sudden attack of fever
Will cause the shark to shiver.

42

The plague will always pass him by,
He neither coughs nor sneezes,
He is the only creature who's
Immune to all diseases.

You may be angry with the shark,
But it's impossible to infect him,
So put away your viruses.
Stop trying to inject him.

Sea Capers

I would swim with dolphins,
I would ride the waves,
And talk with the sea scorpions,
In underwater caves.

I would search the caverns
Where the great sea serpents sleep,
And dive, dive, dive with turtles
To the bottom of the deep.

I would ride a great white shark,
Dance with a giant squid,
Wrestle with a walrus
And defeat him, single-handed.

And if I saw a jellyfish,
In fact, if I saw two,
I'd shake them by the tentacles
And say, "How do you do?"

I would hold hands with an octopus
Cruise with a manatee,
But I'm terrified of water,
And I'm frightened of the sea.

In the sea, the air and the ground

Who'll run too slow from my sharp claws?
Who? Who? Who?

The wild geese are flying straight,
Wings wide, and fleet,

He'll raise his head and strike,
His fangs dripping with venom,

Fish eater
Mouse beater

The octopus has eight legs,
That's more than I would choose,

46

And now he flits from flower to flower,
Humming all day long.

A swift sleeps on the wing,
Now that's a peculiar thing.

I know it's buried here somewhere,
And I'm looking high and low.

I would swim with dolphins,
I would ride the waves,

The next thing you should know about the dogfish,
Is its bite is worse than its bark.

Ideas for reading

Written by Linda Pagett B.Ed (hons), M.Ed
Lecturer and Educational Consultant

Learning objectives: explain how writers use figurative and expressive language to create images and atmosphere; offer reasons and evidence for their views, considering alternative opinions; choose and combine words, images and other features for particular effects

Curriculum links: Citizenship: Choices

Interest words: anaconda, caiman, cockroaches, coyote, walrus, manatee, viruses

Resources: paper and colouring pens

Getting started

This book can be read over two or more reading sessions.

- Discuss what makes something a poem, and ask children if they have any favourite poets or poems and why they like them.

- Read the blurb and look at the cover together. Encourage children to predict the features of the poems inside.

- Turning to the contents page, model yourself choosing a poem. Be critical, e.g. *I'm going to choose "Seaside Bandit" because I want to find out what that might be.*

- Demonstrate reading the chosen poem and give reasons for liking or disliking it, e.g. *I like poems that are funny.*

Reading and responding

- Using the contents pages, encourage children to select and read poems to each other.

- Encourage them to try to guess difficult words together, stressing reading for meaning and other important strategies such as using rhyme cues or decoding for unfamiliar words. Explain that sometimes poets invent their own phrases, e.g. "Slime slider" for slug.

- Demonstrate praising a reading of a poem, e.g. *I like the voices you use*, and encourage children to critique each other.